FAST!

QED Publishing

IAN GRAHAM

The words in **bold** are explained in the Glossary on page 116.

Project Editor: Angela Royston
Designer: Andrew Crowson
Picture Researcher: Maria Joannou

Copyright © QED Publishing 2011

This edition published by
QED Publishing
A Quarto group company
226 City Road
London EC1V 2TT

www.qed-publishing.co.uk

A catalogue record for this book is available from the
British Library.

ISBN 978 1 84835 686 3

Printed in China

Picture credits
(t=top, b=bottom, l=left, r=right, c=centre)
Alamy Images Motoring Picture Library 27tl, Rhys Stacker 27tr,
R A Rayworth 39tl, Jack Sullivan 43tl, Trinity Mirror/Mirrorpix
42–43, Clynt Garnham Transportation 48, Mary Evans Picture
Library 62–63, Justin Prenton 63t, Trinity Mirror/Mirrorpix
76t, 82t, 94–95, Danita Delimont 80–81, EuroStyle Graphics
100–101, Bernard Friel/Danita Delimont 97t, Imagebroker/
Günter Flegar 97c, Barry Bland 97b, UK Alan King 102–103t;
American Challenge, Inc 87b; **Bloodhound SSC** Curventa
31t & c; **Cedar Point Amusement Park** 44; **Corbis** 56–57,
Transtock 8–9, Car Culture 9c, George Tiedemann/GT Images
11t, Car Culture 14, Bettmann 18, 19t, 19b, 22, 23b, 24t, 24–25,
25c, Bettmann 95c, 99t & c, Skyscan 29t, 96–97, Hulton-Deutsch
Collection 35tl & b, Bettmann 40–41, 41tr, Paul Almasy 47bl,
Steve Kaufman 47br, Michel Ginfray/Sygma 50–51, G. Bowater
52–53, Paul Souders 55t, Neil Rabinowitz 81t, Stringer 65tl,
Patrick Durand 72, Denis Balibouse/Reuters 92t, Jean-Christophe
Bott/EPA 92–93, Smithsonian Institution 101c, Paco Campos/
EFE 105t; **Corbis Getty Images** STR/Stringer FC, Science &
Society Picture Library 36t, 36–37, 37c, 43tr, AFP/Stan Honda
45t, AFP/Yoshokazu Tsuno 47t, Superstock 50b, 51bl, Koichi
Kamoshida/Stringer 55br, Ralph Crane/Time Life Pictures 56t;
Department of Defense 65b; **Florida Atlantic University** 65tr;
Getty Images 7bl, 29b, Hulton Archive/H.F. Davis/Stringer
16, Science & Society Picture Library 17t, 66b, Hulton Archive
21b, John Chapple 28–29, Hulton Archive/Stringer 67c, Kos
Picture Source 70, Cate Gillon 71t, AFP/Marcel Mochet 71b,
74–75, AFP/Gerard Julien 74b, Hulton Archive/Central Press/
Stringer 76–77, AFP/Stringer 78t, AFP/Cris Bouroncle 79t, 79c,
AFP/Fabrice Coffrini 93tl, Hulton Archive/Fox Photos/Stringer
94t; **INCAT** Trevor Kidd 73t, Fjord Line 73c; **Library of
Congress** 90–91, 91b; **NASA** 110, 111tl, tr & b, 112, 113tl & tr,
Dryden Flight Research Center 91c, 101t, 106, 107t & b, 108b,
108–109, 109tr, Johnson Space Center Collection 113b, Steve
Lighthill 114–115, 115tr; **National Railway Museum** SSPL 39tr,
82–83, 83tl, 83tr; **North American Eagle, Inc** Rachel Shadle
30; **Photolibrary** National Motor Museum 23t, 25t, 27b, Paul
Nevin 38–39, Photononstop/Alain Marcay 35tr, 52t, Imagestate/
Gordan Nicholson 42t, Japan Travel Bureau 46, Picture Press/
Harald Schoen 49tl, SGM SGM 53tl, Imagebroker.net/Marijan
Murat 53tr, Philip Wallick 102–103b; **Photoshot** UPPA/
Andrew_Gombert 45b, ChinaFotoPress 54t; **Press Association
Images** Nigel Bennetts/PA Archive 73b, Jim Bryant/AP 81c;
QWSR Ltd 87t, 87c; **Reaction Engines Limited** Adrian
Mann 115b; **Rex Features** 51br, 78–79, 93r, Sipa Press 26–27
(background), 75r, 103c, John Curtis 27tc, Daily Mail 66–67,
Phil Rees 71c, Newspix 84t, 86, Rob Judges 102c, **SailRocket**
68–69, 69t, 69bl, 69br; **Scaled Composites, LLC** 109b, Jim
Campbell/Aero-News Network 91t; **Shelby Supercars** 12, 13t,
13b; **Shutterstock** Christoff 9b, AJancso 10, Renkshot 11b,
Holger Mette 54–55, Rodolfo Arpia 67b; **Shutterstock Talgo
(Deutschland) GmbH** 41tl; **Siemens** 49tr; **Top 1 Oil Products
Company** 15t, 15b; **Topham Picturepoint** 7t, 20t, 77t, 77c,
National Motor Museum/HIP 20b, 21t, The Granger Collection
37t, 38t, UPP 84–85, 85t, 2006 Alinari 95t, Flight Collection 98t,
105c, Ullsteinbild 98–99; **U.S. Air Force** 57t, 104–105, 107c,
Senior Airman Vernon Young 104t, Chad Bellay 114b; **U.S. Navy**
64; **Wikimedia Commons** 6, 7br, Brian Snelson 9t, Przemysław
Jahr 17b, HMSO/Crown Copyright 34t & b, Kgrr (cc) 2007 by
Konrad Roeder 49b, AllenS 57c, Alfred John West 63b.
Illustrations on pages 58 and 59 by Leonardo Meschini, based on
graphics courtesy of Discovery Communications

Contents

Note: The vehicles in each section appear in order of speed, from the slowest to the fastest.

SUPERCARS

... and other fast machines on the road

Fastest on wheels

Just over 100 years ago, the fastest cars were slower than a family car today. Now, the world's fastest cars are speedier than a jet airliner.

Never satisfied

One of the oddest record breakers was an **electric car** called *La Jamais Contente*. Its name means 'never satisfied' in French. It was an iron tube with a pointed nose and tail. When scientists saw it, they thought it would go so fast that the driver would not be able to breathe! Luckily, they were wrong. The driver, Camille Jenatzy, set a world record speed of 105 **kilometres** per hour on 29 April 1899, and he lived to tell the tale.

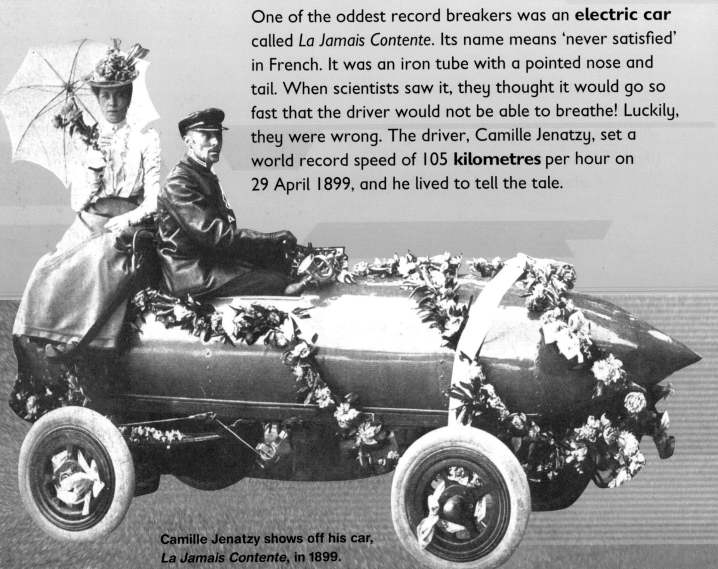

Camille Jenatzy shows off his car, *La Jamais Contente*, in 1899.

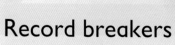

Record breakers

Cars with **gasoline engines** were soon going faster than electric cars. Then, in the 1960s, designers started using **jet engines** to make their cars go even faster. The cars and their drivers became as famous as movie stars are today. Teams of **designers** and **engineers** are now building new cars to set new speed records in the future. The power of engines is measured in **horsepower.**

Crowds gathered to see Malcolm Campbell's latest Bluebird car in January 1935.

In 1997, *Thrust SSC* went faster than the speed of sound. It was powered by two huge jet engines.

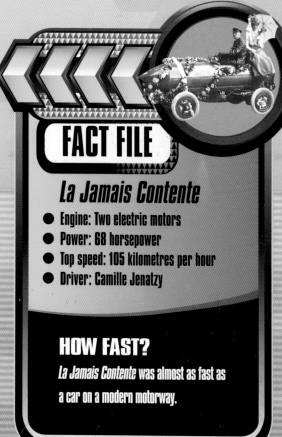

FACT FILE

La Jamais Contente

- Engine: Two electric motors
- Power: 68 horsepower
- Top speed: 105 kilometres per hour
- Driver: Camille Jenatzy

HOW FAST?

La Jamais Contente was almost as fast as a car on a modern motorway.

Classic cars

Some cars are so successful that they become classics. Classics are still great cars, even when they are out of date.

Classic racing car

The Bugatti Type 35 is probably the most successful racing car ever made. It won up to 2000 races in the 1920s and 1930s. Another Italian automobile manufacturer, Ferrari, is one of the most famous names in motor racing. Ferrari also makes sports cars for the road.

The Bugatti Type 35 racing car won the Grand Prix world championship of 1926.

Classic sports cars

The Ferrari 250 GTO, a 1960s sports car, is still thought to be one of the best sports cars ever made. An Italian tractor manufacturer named Ferruccio Lamborghini decided to build his own high-quality fast cars to rival Ferrari. One of his cars, the Lamborghini Diablo, was the fastest road car in the world when it went on sale in 1990.

Only 36 Ferrari 250 GTOs were built to compete in sports car races between 1962 and 1964.

The Lamborghini Diablo's engine is in the middle of the car, behind the driver.

FACT FILE

Lamborghini Diablo

- Engine: 5.7 litres V12
- Power: 492 horsepower
- Top speed: 325 kilometres per hour

HOW FAST?

A Lamborghini Diablo is as fast as a racing car today.

Racing cars

Soon after the first cars were built, people wanted to know which car was the fastest. Cars were soon being built specially for racing.

Open-wheel racers

The top international racing competition is called Formula 1. Racing cars are single-seaters and are also called open-wheel cars. These cars can reach a top speed of about 380 kilometres per hour. In the USA, the IndyCar series is the most popular competition for open-wheel cars.

Open-wheel racing cars have wings at the front and back to help them go around bends faster.

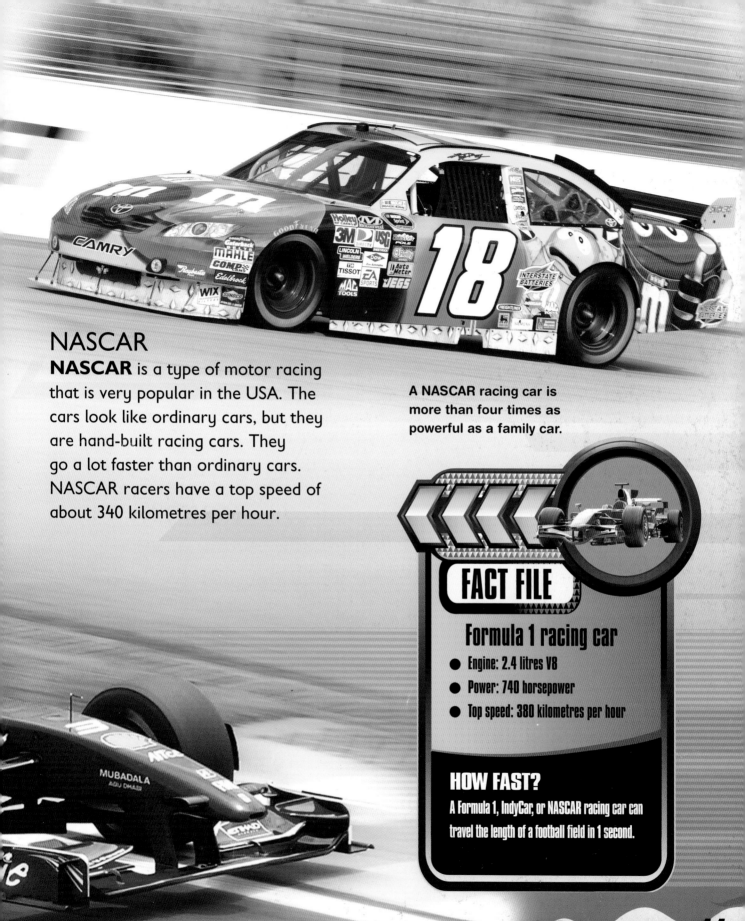

NASCAR

NASCAR is a type of motor racing that is very popular in the USA. The cars look like ordinary cars, but they are hand-built racing cars. They go a lot faster than ordinary cars. NASCAR racers have a top speed of about 340 kilometres per hour.

A NASCAR racing car is more than four times as powerful as a family car.

FACT FILE

Formula 1 racing car

- Engine: 2.4 litres V8
- Power: 740 horsepower
- Top speed: 380 kilometres per hour

HOW FAST?

A Formula 1, IndyCar, or NASCAR racing car can travel the length of a football field in 1 second.

Supercars

A few of the cars that are built for driving on public roads can now go faster than the record-breaking cars of the 1920s. These modern marvels are called supercars.

The fastest supercar

Supercars are made by some of the greatest names in automotive history, including Ferrari, Bugatti, Jaguar, and Lamborghini. The fastest supercar today is the SSC Ultimate Aero TT. Most cars have their engine at the front. The SSC Ultimate Aero TT's **turbocharged** engine is behind the driver. This makes the front of the car lower. Air flows over the car more smoothly, so the car goes faster.

Speed test

On 13 September 2007, the SSC Ultimate Aero TT was tested to prove that it was the fastest supercar. A straight, 19-kilometre long stretch of Highway 221 in the US state of Washington was closed for the test. The car roared down the road at a record speed of 412 kilometres per hour.

The SSC Ultimate Aero TT is made of super-lightweight materials.

The SSC Ultimate Aero TT is very low. It stands just over one metre high.

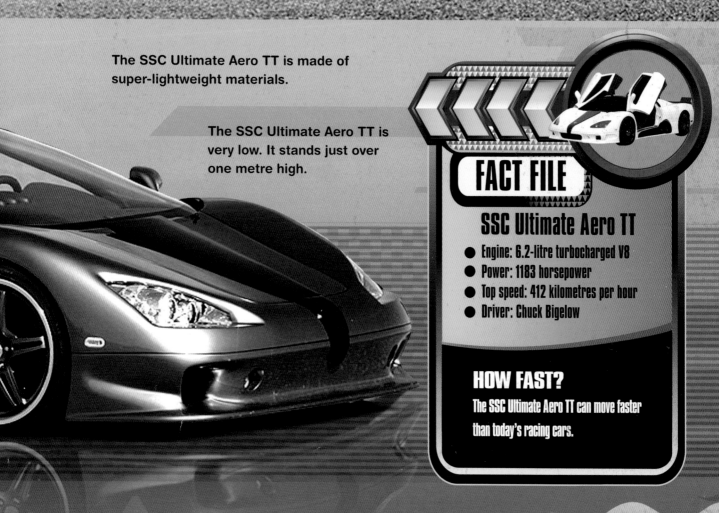

FACT FILE

SSC Ultimate Aero TT

- Engine: 6.2-litre turbocharged V8
- Power: 1183 horsepower
- Top speed: 412 kilometres per hour
- Driver: Chuck Bigelow

HOW FAST?

The SSC Ultimate Aero TT can move faster than today's racing cars.

13

On two wheels

The fastest motorcycles look very different from the motorcycles you see every day. They are called streamliners.

Streamliners

Motorcycles built for breaking speed records don't have to turn corners, or fit in with other traffic. They are designed to do just one thing – go as fast as possible in a straight line. They are so **streamlined** they look like a long, thin tube on wheels. The rider lies down inside the tube.

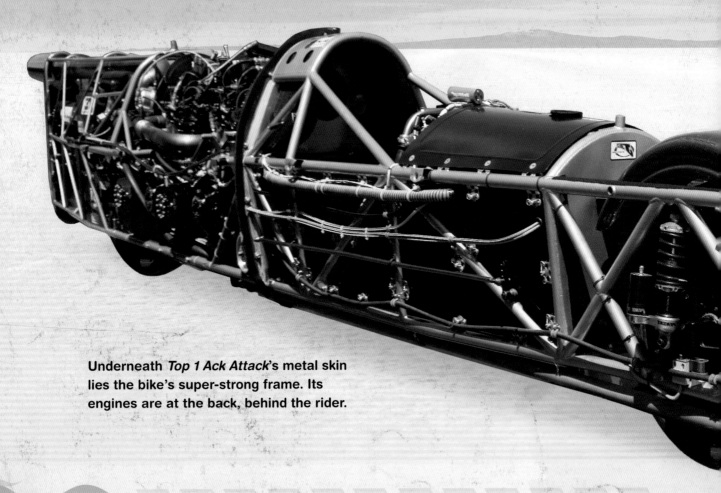

Underneath *Top 1 Ack Attack*'s metal skin lies the bike's super-strong frame. Its engines are at the back, behind the rider.

Top 1 Ack Attack speeds across the Bonneville Salt Flats in the USA.

Top 1 Ack Attack

On 26 September 2008, Rocky Robinson rode his streamliner, called *Top 1 Ack Attack*, to an amazing speed of 580 kilometres per hour. It was faster than any motorcycle had ever gone before. *Top 1 Ack Attack* was so fast because it had two engines working together. Each engine was from a Suzuki Hayabusa, one of the world's fastest motorcycles. Together, they made *Top 1 Ack Attack* unbeatable.

FACT FILE

Top 1 Ack Attack

- Engine: Two Suzuki motorcycle engines
- Power: 800 horsepower
- Top speed: 580 kilometres per hour
- Rider: Rocky Robinson

HOW FAST?

Top 1 Ack Attack went nearly twice as fast as a high-speed train.

Bluebirds

The British racing driver Malcolm Campbell and his son, Donald, set many speed records from the 1920s to the 1960s.

Big engines

When Malcolm Campbell was breaking records, cars were built with bigger engines to make them go faster. Malcolm Campbell's Bluebird cars had giant engines. In those days, anyone who broke the **land speed record** became famous. Campbell became very famous.

The last Bluebird

Donald Campbell built his own record-breaking car. He called it *Bluebird Proteus CN7*. In 1964, he drove his Bluebird to a new land speed record of 648 kilometres per hour. He had also broken the world water speed record earlier the same year. He is still the only person ever to break the land and water speed records in the same year.

Donald Campbell's Bluebird car had a tall tail to keep it going straight at high speed.

Malcolm Campbell and his son Donald stand beside a famous Bluebird car.

FACT FILE

Bluebird Proteus CN7

- Engine: Bristol Siddeley Proteus gas turbine
- Power: 4000 horsepower
- Top speed: 648 kilometres per hour
- Driver: Donald Campbell

HOW FAST?

Bluebird Proteus CN7 travelled twice as fast as a high-speed train goes today.

Spirit of America

In 1963, an American driver named Craig Breedlove surprised everyone by building a car with a jet engine. It looked like a jet plane without wings.

New rules

Record-breaking cars have to follow rules, but there were no rules for **jet-cars**. The rules said that the engine has to drive the car's wheels, but a jet-car's engine doesn't drive the wheels. Instead, the car is pushed along by the jet of air leaving the engine. At first, speed records set by jet-cars were not allowed, but then the rules were changed. Since then, jet-cars have set nearly every land speed record.

Craig Breedlove stands in front of his first jet-car, *Spirit of America*.

Sonic Arrow

Craig Breedlove called his car *Spirit of America*. He drove it at 655 kilometres per hour – faster than any other car in history at that time. He later built another jet-car, *Spirit of America – Sonic 1*. This car went even faster. In 1965, it pushed the record up to 966 kilometres per hour.

Breedlove's second jet-car, *Spirit of America— Sonic 1*, broke the land speed record in 1965.

FACT FILE

Spirit of America—Sonic 1

- Engine: General Electric J79 jet engine
- Power: 17,500 horsepower
- Top speed: 966 kilometres per hour
- Driver: Craig Breedlove

HOW FAST?

Spirit of America – Sonic 1 moved faster than a jet airliner.

Wingfoot Express

After the first *Spirit of America* broke the land speed record, Tom Green and Walt Arfons built *Wingfoot Express*. This was the next jet-car to break the land speed record.

Air speed

Tom Green was very interested in the way air flows around fast cars. He designed the shape of his new car carefully, so that it would move through the air faster than any other car. Walt Arfons built the car's frame and fitted a jet engine to it. Then Green added the specially designed body.

Wingfoot Express arrives at the Bonneville Salt Flats, USA.

Wingfoot Express's driver sits in front of the car's huge jet engine.

FACT FILE

Wingfoot Express

- Engine: Westinghouse J46-WE-8 jet engine
- Power: 10,000 horsepower
- Top speed: 668 kilometres per hour
- Driver: Tom Green

HOW FAST?

Wingfoot Express travelled six times faster than cars on a motorway today.

Salt problems

Wingfoot Express was taken to the Bonneville Salt Flats in the USA, in 1963. This is a dried-up lake with a hard, flat surface of salt. Lots of speed records have been set there. The first time they ran the car, the jet engine sucked in some salt and broke down. Green and Arfons changed the shape of the car to keep this from happening and tried again a year later. This time they were successful. *Wingfoot Express* broke the land speed record.

A rocket-powered *Wingfoot Express* was built, but it was a failure.

The Green Monster

Art Arfons, brother of Walt Arfons, built the record-breaking car the *Green Monster* after he bought himself a jet engine.

The *Green Monster* was powered by a Starfighter jet engine.

Building the monster

The jet engine Art Arfons bought was going cheap, because it was damaged. He repaired the engine and then built a new car around it. He built the car from parts of other cars and trucks. The driver sat in a **cockpit** next to the engine.

The *Green Monster*'s wing held the front of the car down.

Faster and faster

In 1964, Art Arfons showed the world what the *Green Monster* could do. Only three days after *Wingfoot Express* broke the land speed record, the *Green Monster* went even faster. It set a new record of 699 kilometres per hour. It broke the record again in 1965, when it reached 927 kilometres per hour.

FACT FILE

Green Monster

- Engine: General Electric J79 jet engine
- Power: 17,500 horsepower
- Top speed: 927 kilometres per hour
- Driver: Art Arfons

HOW FAST?

The *Green Monster* went about as fast as a jet airliner.

Rocket car

Jets are not the only super-engines that can power a record-breaking car. In 1970, a rocket car smashed the land speed record.

Long and thin

The *Blue Flame* was a **rocket** on wheels. Its long, thin nose held fuel called **liquid natural gas**, or LNG. This was burned by a rocket motor in the car's tail. Instead of taking off like a space rocket, the *Blue Flame* went along the ground very fast.

The *Blue Flame*'s driver, Gary Gabelich, checks out the car.

The *Blue Flame* had a very slim body to go as fast as possible.

The *Blue Flame*'s rocket engine fires amid clouds of smoke.

Driving a rocket

A racing driver named Gary Gabelich was chosen to drive the new rocket car. On 23 October 1970, Gabelich climbed into the car's cockpit, fired the rocket, and drove the *Blue Flame* across the Bonneville Salt Flats to an amazing new land speed record of 1001 kilometres per hour. It was the first time a car had ever set a record faster than 1000 kilometres per hour. *Blue Flame*'s record was not broken for another 13 years.

FACT FILE

Blue Flame

- Engine: RD HP-LNG rocket
- Power: 35,000 horsepower
- Top speed: 1001 kilometres per hour
- Driver: Gary Gabelich

HOW FAST?

A car going as fast as the *Blue Flame* could drive the distance between the North and South poles in less than a day.

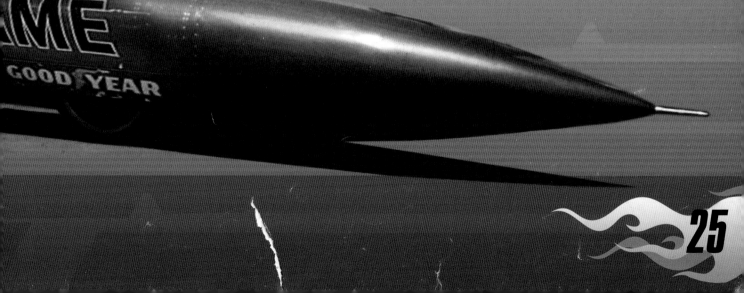

Thrust 2

The work to design and build the next successful land speed record car began in England in 1978. The result was a jet-car called *Thrust 2*.

Straight as an arrow

Thrust 2 was built a little bit like an arrow. Most of its weight was at the front, like the point of an arrow. **Fins** at the back kept the car going in a straight line, as an arrow's feathers do. The wheels were made by hand from solid metal.

Black Rock

Bad weather in the early 1980s made it impossible to run cars at the Bonneville Salt Flats, where land speed records were usually set. The salty ground was too soft. The Black Rock Desert in Nevada was used instead. On 4 October 1983, with Richard Noble at the controls, *Thrust 2* hurtled across the desert. It set a new record of 1019 kilometres per hour.

Thrust 2

- Engine: Rolls-Royce Avon jet engine
- Power: 34,000 horsepower
- Top speed: 1019 kilometres per hour
- Driver: Richard Noble

HOW FAST?

Thrust 2 travels 1 kilometre every 3 seconds.

Thrust 2's land speed record was set by British driver Richard Noble.

Thrust 2 made its first low-speed test runs on rubber tyres.

Faster than sound

A British team decided to build the first supersonic car. It was designed to go faster than the speed of sound, but no one knew if that was possible.

Thrust SSC

The team, led by Richard Noble, named their car *Thrust SSC*. Noble had already driven the *Thrust 2* record-breaking car, but this time he decided that he would run the project and someone else would drive the car. The driver he chose was Andy Green.

***Thrust SSC*'s twin jet engines power it across the desert.**

Two jet engines

Thrust SSC was massive. It weighed 10 tonnes, which is about six or seven times the weight of an ordinary family car. It was powered by two mighty jet engines, side by side. On 15 October 1997, *Thrust SSC* succeeded in setting the first **supersonic** land speed record. This was 50 years and one day after the first supersonic flight by a plane.

Thrust SSC's driver, Andy Green, sits between its two jet engines.

FACT FILE

Thrust SSC

- Engine: Two Rolls-Royce Spey 205 jet engines
- Power: 100,000 horsepower
- Top speed: 1227 kilometres per hour
- Driver: Andy Green

HOW FAST?

Thrust SSC travelled faster on the ground than a jet airliner flies through the air.

Future records

Two new cars are being built to try to break speed records in the future. One is an American car named the *North American Eagle*, and the other is a British car named *Bloodhound SSC*.

Here comes Eagle

North American Eagle is a jet-car that is being designed to set a land speed record of about 1300 kilometres per hour. The bright-red car has a nose like a needle and is powered by an engine from a Starfighter jet fighter plane.

The *North American Eagle* car looks like a fighter plane on wheels.

Bloodhound SSC will make its record attempt in South Africa.

Jet and rocket

Bloodhound SSC is aiming at a much faster record. If it goes as fast as its designers think it should, it will be the first car to reach nearly 1600 kilometres per hour. *Bloodhound SSC's* great speed comes from a jet engine and a rocket. The car will start off by using its jet engine only. When it reaches 480 kilometres per hour, the rocket will fire and boost the car to its amazing top speed.

FACT FILE

Bloodhound SSC

- Engine: A Eurojet EJ200 jet engine and a rocket
- Power: Unknown
- Top speed: 1600 kilometres per hour
- Driver: Andy Green

HOW FAST?

Bloodhound SSC will go as fast as a fighter jet.

BULLET TRAINS

... and other fast machines on rails

Fastest on rails

When the first railroads were built 200 years ago, it was faster to ride on horseback than to take a train. Soon, trains overtook horses and the train became the fastest way to travel.

The first steam train

In 1804, Richard Trevithick built the world's first successful **locomotive** powered by steam. Trevithick's locomotive pulled coal wagons at the Penydarren ironworks in Wales, but it wasn't fast. It took four hours to haul 10 tonnes of coal 16 kilometres, but it proved that locomotives could pull heavy loads.

The Penydarren locomotive ran on thin, flat iron rails.

The large wheel on Richard Trevithick's Penydarren locomotive helped the engine run smoothly.

Locomotion

- Type: Steam
- Country: United Kingdom
- Top speed: 24 kilometres per hour

HOW FAST?

Locomotion went about five times faster than a person walking.

High-speed trains provide fast intercity travel.

Going faster

In 1825, George and Robert Stephenson built a locomotive, called *Locomotion*. It too carried coal, but was six times faster than Trevithick's locomotive. Today, high-speed trains carry passengers at speeds as fast as racing cars. **Experimental** trains go even faster.

Stephenson's *Locomotion* was in service until 1841.

Rocket

A steam locomotive called *Rocket* was built specially for a competition in 1829. It proved to be the best and the fastest.

Rocket was built specially for the Rainhill Trials.

The Rainhill Trials

While the Liverpool and Manchester Railway was being built in England in the 1820s, a competition was held to find the best locomotive to pull its trains. Five locomotives took part in the competition, which was called the Rainhill Trials. Thousands of people lined the tracks to see the trains.

ROCKET

A clear winner

The Trials went on for eight days. Most of the locomotives broke down, but *Rocket* kept going and was the clear winner. It was built by George Stephenson and his son, Robert. *Rocket* reached a top speed of 48 kilometres per hour and managed to haul a load weighing more than 13 tonnes.

George Stephenson prepares *Rocket* for its run in the Rainhill Trials.

This is an exact copy of *Rocket*. It was built to show people what the first trains were like.

FACT FILE

Rocket

- **Type:** Steam
- **Country:** United Kindgom
- **Top speed:** 48 kilometres per hour

HOW FAST?

Rocket went about as fast as cars are allowed to travel in towns.

Flying Scotsman

Several trains are said to have set speed records in the 1890s and early 1900s, but no one could be sure if the records were correct. To solve this problem, trains started carrying equipment for measuring their speeds when they tried to break records.

Empire State Express ran between New York City and Buffalo in the 1890s.

Early claims

In 1893, a U.S. locomotive named *Empire State Express No.999* was said to have reached 180 kilometres per hour. In 1904, a British locomotive called *City of Truro* was said to have gone faster than 160 kilometres per hour. However, these trains did not have speed-recording equipment on board, so no one knows exactly how fast they really went.

Flying Scotsman toured Australia in 1989.

City of Truro steams through Wales.

Official record

On 30 November 1934, a British locomotive called *Flying Scotsman* carried equipment on board to measure its speed. The equipment measured its speed at 160 kilometres per hour, the first **official** rail speed record.

FACT FILE

Flying Scotsman

- Type: Steam
- Country: United Kingdom
- Top speed: 160 kilometres per hour

HOW FAST?

Flying Scotsman carried passengers between London and Edinburgh in just eight hours.

Pioneer Zephyr

In the 1930s, railroad bosses in the USA were looking for ways to persuade more people to travel by train. The Chicago, Burlington and Quincy Railroad built a fantastic new train, which was powered by a diesel engine.

Pioneer Zephyr speeds to a world record.

Train from the future

The gleaming silver-coloured *Pioneer Zephyr* looked like a train from the future. On 26 May 1934, it made a 'dawn-to-dusk dash' from Denver to Chicago. All other trains were cleared out of its way. During the 1633-kilometre journey, *Pioneer Zephyr* reached a new world record speed of 181 kilometre per hour.

A Talgo XXI is the fastest diesel train today.

The diesel record

The speeds of **diesel trains** have increased steadily over the years. On 10 July 2002, a Talgo XXI diesel train reached 256 kilometres per hour on a test track in Spain. It was faster than any diesel train had ever gone.

FACT FILE

Pioneer Zephyr
- Type: Diesel
- Country: USA
- Top speed: 181 kilometres per hour

HOW FAST?

Pioneer Zephyr moved as fast as a high-speed police chase.

Mallard

In the 1930s, more and more people were driving cars, and some were already travelling by air. Railroad companies tried to keep passengers travelling by train by showing how fast and reliable trains were.

Mallard **was an A4 Pacific Class steam locomotive.**

Mallard

The London and North Eastern Railway (LNER) company decided to build new, faster trains. The result was a series of streamlined steam locomotives called A4s. One of these new locomotives, named *Mallard*, made history.

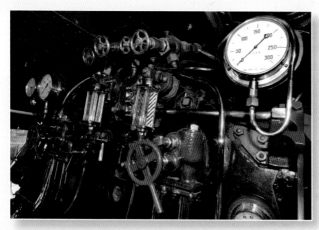

Mallard was controlled by a complicated set of levers and valves.

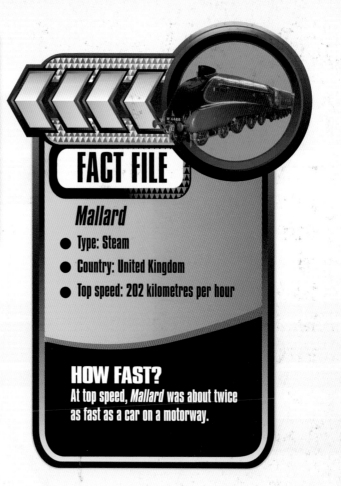

The last steam record

On 3 July 1938, *Mallard* set off with a team of engineers who thought they were doing some ordinary tests. When they were on board, they were told that the train was going to try to break the world rail speed record. Speed-recording equipment had already been loaded onto the train. *Mallard* reached a record-breaking speed of 202 kilometres per hour. This is still the world record for a steam train.

Mallard's wedge-shaped nose helped it go faster than any other steam train.

4468   L N E R

Roller coasters

Roller coasters use rail tracks to give an exciting ride. The cars on the most recent roller coasters speed around twists, turns and loops. Some roller coasters are very fast.

The top thrill

In the 1970s, the fastest roller coasters had a top speed of about 100 kilometres per hour. New roller coasters went faster and faster. When the *Top Thrill Dragster* roller coaster opened in Ohio in 2003, it became the world's fastest. Its cars reached a top speed of 190 kilometres per hour.

The *Top Thrill Dragster* track snakes up and down a tower as tall as a skyscraper.

The fastest ride

Top Thrill Dragster held the record for two years until *Kingda Ka* opened in New Jersey. Its **launch system** boosts the cars to a top speed of 206 kilometres per hour in only 3.5 seconds. The system sends them climbing up a tower 139 metres high – as tall as a 45-floor building. This makes *Kingda Ka* the tallest roller coaster, as well as the fastest.

FACT FILE

Kingda Ka

- Type: Roller coaster
- Country: USA
- Top speed: 206 kilometres per hour

HOW FAST?

Kingda Ka is as fast as a sports car.

Kingda Ka is the tallest and fastest roller coaster.

Bullet trains

The first high-speed electric passenger trains were built in Japan. They quickly became known as 'bullet trains', because their nose is shaped like a bullet.

Special tracks

The first bullet trains in the 1960s ran at 210 kilometres per hour. They held several world speed records. Today, the latest bullet trains run at about 300 kilometres per hour and even faster trains are being designed. They run on special tracks that are as straight and level as possible. Tight bends and uneven tracks would slow the trains down.

The 500 Series bullet train was introduced in 1997.

High voltage

The trains have up to 14 passenger cars and can be 400 metres long. Their **electric motors** are powered from 25,000-**volt** cables hanging above the track. Earthquakes are common in Japan. If the tracks are shaken by a strong earthquake, the trains stop **automatically** and safely.

Japan's bullet trains run on special high-speed tracks.

Japan's original 0 Series bullet trains ran from 1964 until 2008.

FACT FILE

N700 Shinkansen train
- Type: Electric
- Country: Japan
- Top speed: 300 kilometres per hour

HOW FAST?
The fastest bullet trains are as fast as a racing car at top speed.

High-speed trains

Japan's bullet trains showed the rest of the world the future of passenger rail travel. In the following 30 years, a number of new high-speed electric railroads were built in other countries.

High-speed rail

The French TGV came first in 1981. Then Germany built its ICE trains. They have been carrying passengers since 1989. Spain's AVE came next in 1992. Then in 2000, the Acela Express started running between Boston and Washington, D.C. It tilts as it goes around bends to make the journey smoother.

Germany's ICE (InterCity Express) trains run at up to 300 kilometres per hour.

FACT FILE

AVE Class 103
- Type: Electric
- Country: Spain
- Top speed: 403 kilometres per hour

HOW FAST?
The AVE class 103's record-breaking top speed is more than four times faster than a car on a motorway.

Spain's AVE 103 is the world's fastest passenger train.

Spanish record
A Spanish AVE Class 103 train broke the record for the fastest passenger train on 16 July 2006. It reached a speed of 403 kilometres per hour while travelling between Madrid and Zaragoza. Special record-breaking trains have gone faster, but this was an ordinary passenger train.

The Acela Express carries more than 3 million passengers a year.

Air trains

Different train-makers have tried to build trains that glide on a cushion of air. There have been 'air train' projects in the USA and France.

Aerotrain

In the 1950s, the U.S. General Motors car company built the Aerotrain. Its diesel locomotive looked like a 1950s motor car. The passenger cars sat on bags full of air. The air-bags were supposed to give passengers a smoother ride. However, when the trains neared their top speed, the cars bounced around uncomfortably.

Only two Aerotrains were ever built.

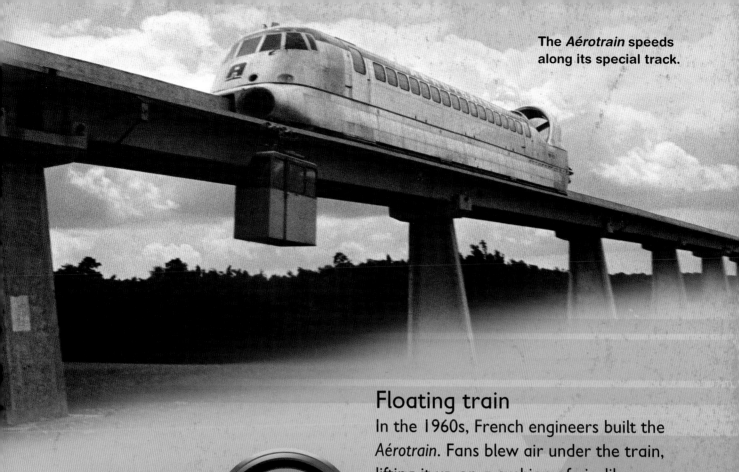

The *Aérotrain* speeds along its special track.

Floating train

In the 1960s, French engineers built the *Aérotrain*. Fans blew air under the train, lifting it up on a cushion of air, like a hovercraft. A spinning **propeller** pushed the train along the track. **Prototypes** were tested and reached 430 kilometres per hour, but the *Aérotrain* project did not go any further.

FACT FILE

Aérotrain

● Type: Hovertrain
● Country: France
● Top speed: 430 kilometres per hour

HOW FAST?

The French *Aérotrain* would easily win a race against any racing car today.

This rocket-powered *Aérotrain* reached a speed of 345 kilometres per hour in 1966.

TGV

The TGV was the first high-speed train built in Europe after Japan's bullet trains. It set a series of speed records.

Radio signals

TGV trains run on high-speed tracks throughout France and in some nearby countries. The trains go so fast that the drivers can't see signals alongside the track. Instead, signal information is sent by radio into the driver's cab.

A TGV power car is immensely powerful.

A TGV Atlantique train speeds through the French countryside.

A TGV train is powered by electricity.

FACT FILE

TGV

- Type: Electric
- Country: France
- Top speed: 574 kilometres per hour

HOW FAST?

The record-breaking TGV went as fast as a World War II fighter.

Super-TGV

TGVs travel at up to 320 kilometres per hour, but one TGV went a lot faster. It was shorter than usual, and the electric cable above the track supplied the train with 31,000 volts instead of the usual 25,000. This train was more than twice as powerful as a normal TGV. On 3 April 2007, it set a record speed for passenger trains of 574 kilometres per hour.

Flying trains

The fastest trains fly above their track! Without wheels rolling on rails, they can go a lot faster. These trains are called maglevs.

Maglevs run on tracks that are called guideways.

Magnetic trains

A maglev is a magnetic levitation train. The train and its special track are both magnetic. When two magnets are brought close together, they either snap together or push each other apart. Maglevs use the push of this powerful magnetic force to lift a whole train off the ground.

This German high-speed train, called *Transrapid*, is a maglev.

Chinese maglev

The first passenger-carrying maglev opened for business in Shanghai, China, in 2004. The trains, which were designed in Germany, usually travel at up to 350 kilometres per hour between the city of Shanghai and its international airport. One train reached 501 kilometres per hour in a test run in 2003. Experimental maglevs have gone even faster. In 2003, a Japanese experimental maglev called *MLX01* reached a world record speed of 581 kilometres per hour.

The Shanghai maglev approaches a station.

FACT FILE

MLX01

- Type: Maglev
- Country: Japan
- Top speed: 581 kilometres per hour

HOW FAST?

Japan's *MLX01* maglev goes at more than half the speed of a jet airliner.

Rocket sleds

The fastest rail vehicles are rocket sleds. A rocket sled is a vehicle fired along a rail at great speed by rockets.

High-speed tests

Rocket sleds are used to test the shape of high-speed vehicles, such as aircraft, **missiles** and cars that set land speed records. A **model** of the vehicle, or just its nose, is bolted to the sled and fired down the rail. Cameras alongside the track show what happens to the model.

Technicians prepare a rocket sled for a test firing.

Part of a missile is boosted to a high speed by a rocket sled during a test.

In the 1950s, people rode on rocket sleds to test the effects on the body.

Fastest ever

The highest speed ever reached by a rocket sled is 10,604 kilometres per hour. It's the world record speed for any rail vehicle, ever. The record was set on 31 January 2008, at the Holloman Air Force Base in New Mexico. The track is called the High-Speed Test Track. It is 15,480 metres long and perfectly straight. It is used to test parachutes, the shape of new rockets, new types of aircraft engine, and **ejection seats**.

FACT FILE

Holloman Air Force Base Test Track

- Type: Rocket sled track
- Country: USA
- Top speed: 10,604 kilometres per hour

HOW FAST?

The Holloman rocket sled can travel the length of 32 football fields every second!

Future records

Imagine boarding a train in London and going non-stop to New York City in less than an hour! Some engineers think it might be possible to do this!

Atlantic tunnel

The plan is to send ultra-high-speed trains through a railway tunnel that floats just under the surface of the Atlantic Ocean. Cables **anchored** to the ocean floor would hold the tunnel in position. Inside the tunnel, maglev trains would travel at almost 8000 kilometres per hour, or nearly ten times faster than a jet airliner.

Cables would hold this futuristic tunnel in place under the water.

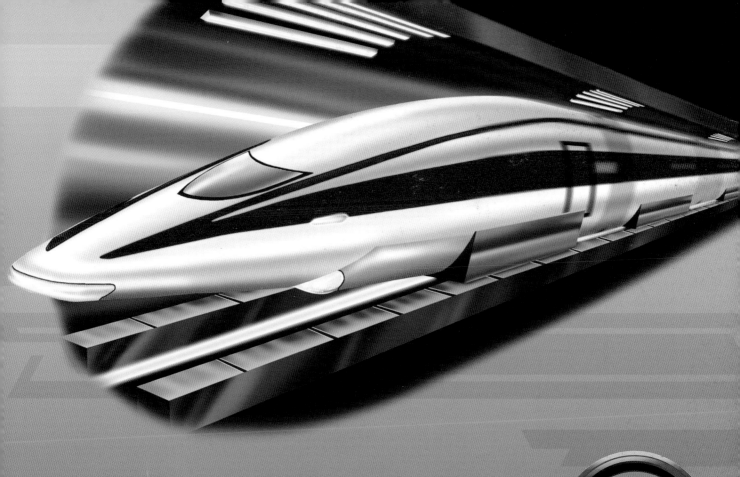

An artist's impression of a maglev train flying through the underwater tunnel.

Airtight train

A train travelling at such a high speed would be slowed down too much by air in the tunnel, so the air would have to be taken out of the tunnel. The train would be sealed, so it would need its own air supply for the people inside to breathe, like a spaceship. No one knows if this amazing project will ever be built.

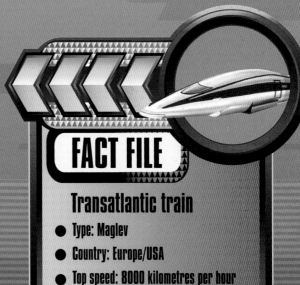

FACT FILE

Transatlantic train

- **Type: Maglev**
- **Country: Europe/USA**
- **Top speed: 8000 kilometres per hour**

HOW FAST?

The transatlantic maglev would be 20 times faster than a passenger train today.

SPEEDBOATS

. . . and other fast machines in the water

Fastest in the water

The first speed records on water were set by boats with steam engines. Boats have been getting faster ever since.

Turbinia's long slender hull sliced through the water easily.

Turbinia

In 1894, the fastest boat in the world was called *Turbinia*. It was the first boat with a **steam turbine engine**. The spinning turbine turned the boat's propeller. *Turbinia* impressed Britain's Royal Navy so much that they decided to power all new warships with steam turbine engines.

Jet-powered hydroplanes are the fastest boats.

Speeding up

In the 1920s, racing boats set faster and faster records. Today, there are **jet-powered** boats and boats that fly above the water! The fastest boats are **hydroplanes** that skim the waves at faster speeds than a jet airliner! The power of a boat's engine is measured in horsepower.

FACT FILE

Turbinia

● Length: 31.6 metres
● Weight: 45 tonnes
● Engine: Steam turbine
● Power: 2000 horsepower
● Top speed: 63 kilometres per hour
● Crew: Unknown

HOW FAST?

Turbinia moved more than twice as fast as a modern oil tanker.

Under the waves

Submarines can go faster under the water than on top of it. Waves on the surface slow them down. When they dive, they pick up speed because the water flows around them more smoothly.

Fast subs

The first of the fast, modern submarines was the US Navy's *Albacore*. Its **hull** was shaped like a teardrop so that it slipped through the water very easily. This submarine had a top speed of 61 kilometres per hour underwater. Russian Akula class submarines are even faster.

The USS *Albacore* was launched in 1953.

FACT FILE

Akula class submarine

- Length: 110 metres
- Weight: up to 6,800 tonnes
- Engine: Nuclear
- Power: 43,000 horsepower
- Top speed: 65 kilometres per hour
- Crew: 62

HOW FAST?

A Russian Akula class submarine travels the length of a football field in less than six seconds.

Talon-1 is a human-powered submarine propelled by a diver inside it.

Muscle power

Races are held every year to find the fastest human-powered submarine. One or two divers inside each submarine pedal to turn the propeller! The 2009 International Submarine Races were won by *Talon-1* at a speed of 11.6 kilometres per hour, three or four times faster than walking speed.

Russian Akula class submarines are very fast underwater and also very quiet.

Fastest liner

The Blue Riband is an honor given to the fastest passenger liner to cross the Atlantic Ocean in regular passenger service.

Super Sirius

The Blue Riband has been held by 23 British ships, 3 German, 3 American, 1 Italian and 1 French. The first holder of the Blue Riband was a British paddle steamer called *Sirius* in 1838. Its steam engine turned a big paddle wheel on each side of the ship. At that time, a **transatlantic** voyage took up to 40 days, but *Sirius* made the crossing in just 18 days.

Sirius had to burn all of its fuel supply of coal, and also some furniture to finish its Atlantic crossing.

SS *United States* was launched in 1952 and immediately became the fastest transatlantic liner.

The United States

The last of the great passenger liners to hold the Blue Riband was the SS *United States*. It was nearly five times longer than *Sirius* and 24 times heavier, but it was much faster. In 1952, it crossed the ocean in only three and a half days – more than four times faster than *Sirius*.

FACT FILE

SS *United States*

- Length: 302 metres
- Weight: 43,000 tonnes
- Engine: Four steam turbines
- Power: 248,000 horsepower
- Top speed: 70 kilometres per hour
- Crew: 900

HOW FAST?

SS *United States* crossed the Atlantic Ocean as fast as a racing cyclist.

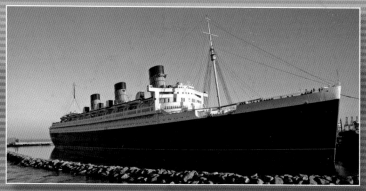

The British liner RMS *Queen Mary* held the Blue Riband for the fastest Atlantic crossing from 1938 until 1952.

Super skimmer

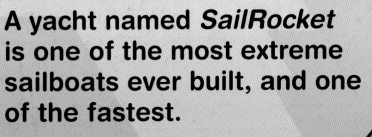

A yacht named *SailRocket* is one of the most extreme sailboats ever built, and one of the fastest.

Beam boat

This strange-looking yacht has a sail at one end of a long beam and a cockpit at the other end. The pilot sits in the cockpit and pushes pedals to control the sail and **rudders**.

SailRocket's sail is held at exactly the right angle to give the fastest speed.

Flying sail

SailRocket's sail stands on a **float**. As the boat speeds up, the float lifts out of the water. The sail flies along, and the cockpit skims across the surface of the water. At top speed, the rudders lift out of the water to make the boat go even faster. On 4 December 2008, its speed was measured at a record-breaking 87.6 kilometres per hour.

The sail is made of stiff material so that it stays in the perfect shape.

The pilot's helmet is shaped like this to help him cut through the wind.

FACT FILE

SailRocket

- Length: 11 metres
- Weight: 140 kilograms
- Engine: None
- Power: Wind power
- Top speed: 87.6 kilometres per hour
- Crew: 1

HOW FAST?

At top speed, *SailRocket* travels the same length as a football field in just 4 seconds.

Round the world

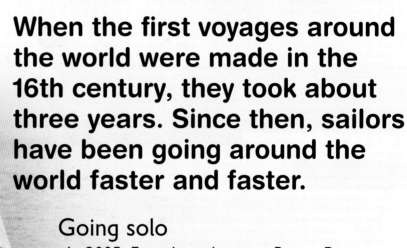

When the first voyages around the world were made in the 16th century, they took about three years. Since then, sailors have been going around the world faster and faster.

Going solo

In 2005, French yachtsman, Bruno Peyron, set a round-the-world record of 50 days. His yacht, *Orange II*, had a crew of 13. In 2007, another French yachtsman, Francis Joyon, broke the record for sailing around the world on his own. He made the solo voyage in his yacht *IDEC II* in 57 days.

The record-breaking yacht *Orange II* is a catamaran – it has two hulls.

Earthrace was powered by two diesel engines.

Earthrace

In 2008, a powerboat called *Earthrace* circled the world in 61 days. This was a record time for powerboats. *Earthrace* is a trimaran — it has three hulls. Two small hulls keep the bigger middle hull steady in the water.

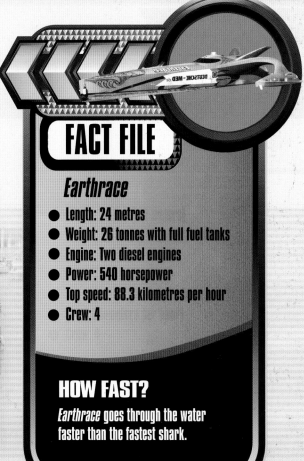

FACT FILE

Earthrace

- Length: 24 metres
- Weight: 26 tonnes with full fuel tanks
- Engine: Two diesel engines
- Power: 540 horsepower
- Top speed: 88.3 kilometres per hour
- Crew: 4

HOW FAST?

Earthrace goes through the water faster than the fastest shark.

IDEC II was designed to be sailed very fast by only one person.

Crossing the Atlantic

The Hales Trophy is awarded to any kind of passenger ship that makes the fastest crossing of the Atlantic Ocean. A ship can win the trophy even if it does not normally cross the Atlantic.

Water jets

In 1990, an ocean-going passenger ship named *Hoverspeed Great Britain* crossed the ocean in a record time of 3 days 7 hours 54 minutes. It was powered by waterjet engines. They suck in seawater and pump it out behind the ship at high speed.

Hoverspeed Great Britain's slim hulls slice easily through the waves.

Catalonia was later renamed *Express*. It carries 225 cars and 877 passengers.

Cat Link V

In 1998, a bigger passenger ship named *Catalonia* broke the transatlantic record, but the new record stood for only six weeks. It was broken by *Cat Link V*, the first commercial passenger vessel to cross the Atlantic Ocean in less than three days. During the record-breaking crossing, it stopped to help search for a missing plane, but still made the crossing in 2 days 20 hours!

FACT FILE

Cat Link V

- Length: 91 metres
- Weight: 510 tonnes
- Engine: Four marine diesel engines
- Power: 34,000 horsepower
- Top speed: 89 kilometres per hour
- Crew: Unknown

HOW FAST?

Cat Link V is about 1.5 times faster than a naval destroyer.

Cat Link V was renamed *Fjord Cat*. It is the world's fastest passenger vessel.

Flying yacht

The fastest sailboat in the world flies above the water! Flying over the waves, instead of pushing through them, makes a boat go faster.

Underwater wings

When a yacht named *l'Hydroptère* is sitting still in the water, it looks like a normal sailing boat, but hidden below it are underwater wings called foils. They work like aircraft wings. As the yacht speeds up, the foils 'fly' through the water. They slowly raise the boat higher and higher, until its whole hull is out of the water.

L'Hydroptère takes off as it picks up speed and its underwater foils start to work.

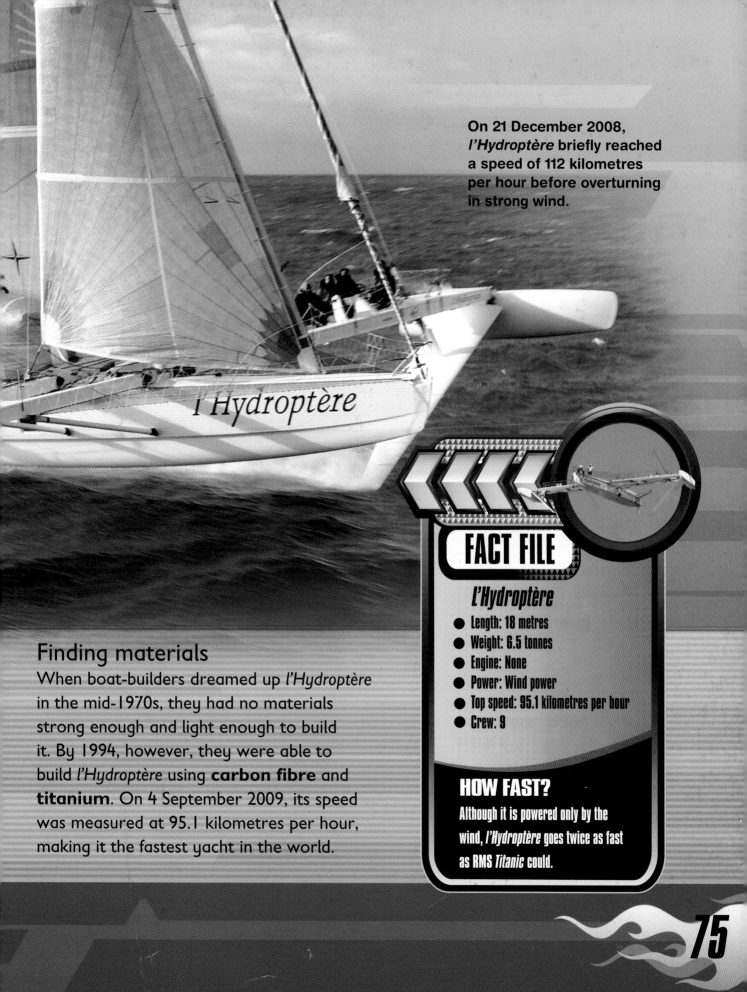

On 21 December 2008, *l'Hydroptère* briefly reached a speed of 112 kilometres per hour before overturning in strong wind.

Finding materials

When boat-builders dreamed up *l'Hydroptère* in the mid-1970s, they had no materials strong enough and light enough to build it. By 1994, however, they were able to build *l'Hydroptère* using **carbon fibre** and **titanium**. On 4 September 2009, its speed was measured at 95.1 kilometres per hour, making it the fastest yacht in the world.

FACT FILE

l'Hydroptère
- Length: 18 metres
- Weight: 6.5 tonnes
- Engine: None
- Power: Wind power
- Top speed: 95.1 kilometres per hour
- Crew: 9

HOW FAST?
Although it is powered only by the wind, *l'Hydroptère* goes twice as fast as RMS *Titanic* could.

75

Bluebirds

After breaking the land speed record for the last time in 1935, British racing driver, Malcolm Campbell turned his attention to the world water speed record.

Bluebird K3

Bluebird K3 was Campbell's first record-breaking boat. This type of boat is called a hydroplane. It goes fast by skimming across the water's surface. *Bluebird K3* was powered by an aircraft engine. On 1 September 1937, Campbell set a water speed record of 203 kilometres per hour on Lake Maggiore in Switzerland. He broke his own record twice more.

Malcolm Campbell wore little protective clothing – just a pair of goggles and a lifejacket.

Campbell sits in the cockpit in front of *Bluebird K3*'s huge engine.

Bluebird K4

To go even faster, Campbell had a new boat built. *Bluebird K4* used the same engine as *K3*, but the boat was a different shape. On 19 August 1939, Campbell set his last, and fastest, water speed record of 228 kilometres per hour on an English lake called Coniston Water.

Campbell set a new speed record in *Bluebird K3* on Lake Hallwyl in Switzerland, in 1938.

FACT FILE

Bluebird K4

- Length: 8.3 metres
- Weight: 2.5 tonnes
- Engine: Rolls-Royce R-Type aircraft engine
- Power: 2500 horsepower
- Top speed: 228 kilometres per hour
- Crew: 1

HOW FAST?

Bluebird K4 was twice as fast as a car on a motorway.

Powerboat racers

Big powerboats race each other across the sea. Today's powerboats are faster than Malcolm Campbell's Bluebirds.

Two hulls

The fastest sea-going racers are Class 1 Powerboats. These racing boats have two hulls, one next to the other. Boats with two hulls are called catamarans. There is an engine in the tail end of each hull. Each boat has a crew of two. The crew members wear **fireproof** overalls and helmets, like auto-racing drivers.

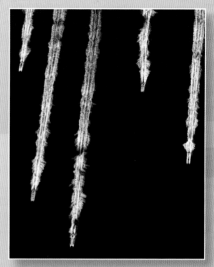

Class 1 powerboats race through the water, leaving foaming trails behind them.

A Class 1 powerboat is up to 14 metres long and weighs 5 tonnes.

Ocean-going racers are ten times more powerful than a family car.

Faster and faster

In the 1960s, powerboats could win a race with a speed of 50 kilometres per hour. In the 1980s, they were reaching speeds of more than 160 kilometres per hour. Nowadays, a winning boat often speeds across the water at more than 200 kilometres per hour.

FACT FILE

Victory 1 (Class 1 Powerboat)

- Length: 12.7 metres
- Weight: 4.8 tonnes
- Engines: Two Victory V12s
- Power: 1800 horsepower
- Top speed: 255 kilometres per hour
- Crew: 2

HOW FAST?

At top speed, a Class 1 Powerboat could cross the English Channel in 10 minutes, a journey that usually takes 90 minutes by car ferry.

Propeller boats

The last boat with a propeller to break the world water speed record was called *Slo-Mo-Shun IV*, but it wasn't a slow-motion boat.

Smashing records

On 26 June 1950, *Slo-Mo-Shun IV* smashed the water speed record with a speed of 258 kilometres per hour. Two years later, it raised the record to 287 kilometres per hour. After *Slo-Mo-Shun IV*, jet-powered boats took over as the world's fastest boats, so a separate record was set up for boats with propellers. In 2000, a propeller-driven boat called *Miss Freei* set a record of 330 kilometres per hour.

In 2000, *Miss Freei* broke a speed record that had stood for 38 years.

Miss Budweiser's cockpit cover is from an F-16 fighter plane.

Miss Budweiser

In 2004, *Miss Budweiser* pushed the record for propeller-driven boats up to 354 kilometres per hour. *Miss Budweiser* is powered by a helicopter engine. The engine spins the propeller 10,000 times a minute.

FACT FILE

Miss Budweiser

- Length: 9.1 metres
- Weight: 2.5 tonnes
- Engine: Lycoming turbine
- Power: 2650 horsepower
- Top speed: 354 kilometres per hour
- Crew: 1

HOW FAST?

Miss Budweiser can move as fast as a Formula 1 racing car.

The last Bluebird

Donald Campbell, the son of Malcolm Campbell (see page 76), built a new jet-powered boat to break the world water speed record.

Donald Campbell takes a break before his final record attempt in 1967.

Twice as fast

Donald Campbell's boat was called *Bluebird K7*. Between 1955 and 1964, he broke the water speed record seven times — more than anyone else. He raised the record to 444 kilometres per hour, nearly double his father's last record.

Donald Campbell's *Bluebird K7* jet-boat was the first to go faster than 300 kilometres per hour.

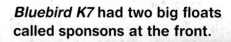

Bluebird K7 had two big floats called sponsons at the front.

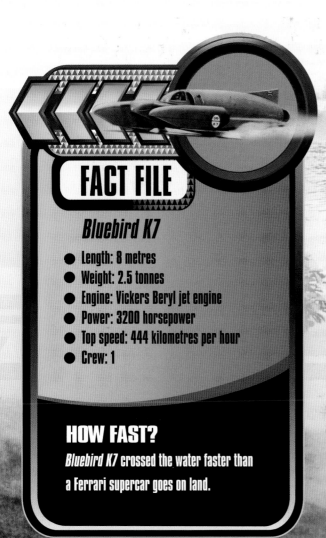

FACT FILE

Bluebird K7

- Length: 8 metres
- Weight: 2.5 tonnes
- Engine: Vickers Beryl jet engine
- Power: 3200 horsepower
- Top speed: 444 kilometres per hour
- Crew: 1

HOW FAST?

Bluebird K7 crossed the water faster than a Ferrari supercar goes on land.

The final challenge

On 4 January 1967, *Bluebird K7* hurtled across Coniston Water at 477 kilometres per hour. To set a new record, the boat had to turn around and come back. Campbell was supposed to stop for fuel, but he didn't.

He started his trip back down the lake. At top speed, the boat hit ripples in the water caused by the first run. The ripples raised *Bluebird*'s nose and it took off. It flipped over and crashed into the water. Campbell died instantly.

Spirit of Australia

On 8 October 1978, Australian powerboat racer, Ken Warby broke the world water speed record with a jet-boat he built in his backyard in Sydney.

A tale of a tail

When Warby tested a model of his boat, he discovered that it would take off if it went faster than 400 kilometres per hour! He changed the design, and added a tail from a plane. These changes kept the boat from taking off. Warby broke the water speed record – and lived to tell the tale!

Ken Warby gets ready to begin testing his boat *Spirit of Australia*.

Spirit of Australia

Warby called his boat *Spirit of Australia*. In 1977, he set a new speed record of 464 kilometres per hour at Blowering Dam in New South Wales, Australia. He thought *Spirit of Australia* could go even faster. He went back to Blowering Dam the following year and raised his own record to 511 kilometres per hour.

Warby sets his first world water speed record in 1977.

Future records

By 2010, Ken Warby's water speed record had stood unbroken for nearly 32 years. Two boats being designed now may challenge Warby's record one day.

Aussie Spirit

In the late 1990s, Ken Warby built a new boat called *Aussie Spirit* to try to break his own record. Then in 2007, at the age of 68, Warby decided to retire. Until someone else goes faster, he will be the fastest person ever on water.

Ken Warby's new boat, *Aussie Spirit*, was completed in 1999.

Quicksilver will be powered by a 10,000 horsepower jet engine.

Challengers

A British boat called *Quicksilver* could become the most powerful boat to try to break the world water speed record. Another boat, called the *American Challenge*, is being built in the United States. Both boats would be made of the latest materials used for planes and spacecraft.

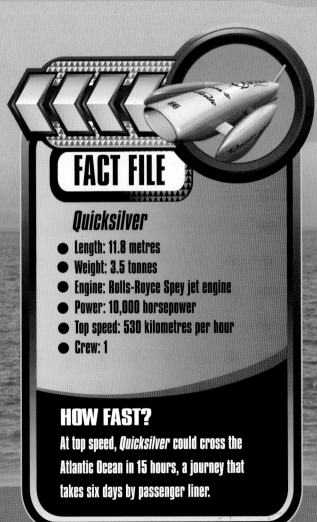

FACT FILE

Quicksilver

- Length: 11.8 metres
- Weight: 3.5 tonnes
- Engine: Rolls-Royce Spey jet engine
- Power: 10,000 horsepower
- Top speed: 530 kilometres per hour
- Crew: 1

HOW FAST?

At top speed, *Quicksilver* could cross the Atlantic Ocean in 15 hours, a journey that takes six days by passenger liner.

American Challenge will be powered by two jet engines.

JET PLANES

... and other fast machines in the air

Fastest in the air

The first planes struggled into the air for just a few seconds. Today, there are jet planes that travel faster than sound and rocket-planes that can fly into space and back.

The first plane

The first plane powered by an engine was called *Flyer*. It was built by two brothers, Orville and Wilbur Wright. In 1903, with Orville at the controls, it flew for just 12 seconds. It was the fastest plane in the world, because it was the only plane in the world!

The *Wright Flyer* takes off for the first-ever powered flight.

Faster and faster

Flyer's success showed that powered flight was possible. Other people then quickly started to build their own planes. As the engines became more powerful, the planes became faster and faster. Pilots raced against each other and competed to set new air speed records.

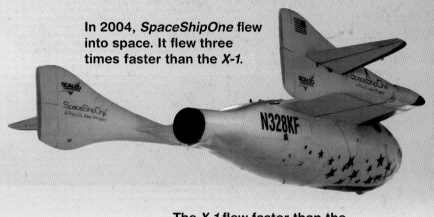

In 2004, *SpaceShipOne* flew into space. It flew three times faster than the *X-1*.

The *X-1* flew faster than the speed of sound in 1947.

FACT FILE

Wright Flyer

- Wingspan: 12.3 metres
- Engine: Wright engine
- Power: 12 horsepower
- Top speed: 15.7 kilometres per hour
- Crew: 1

HOW FAST?
The *Wright Flyer* flew about as fast as someone running along the ground.

Jet-man

Swiss pilot, Yves Rossy was used to flying fighters and airliners. He also dreamed of flying through the air on his own, like Superman.

Rossy's wing has two jet engines on each side.

Four jets

Rossy had a special wing made using carbon fibre. Then, he added four jet engines of the kind that usually power a large model aircraft. In 2006, he strapped the wing to his back and jumped out of a plane. Then, he started the jet engines and flew on his own for the first time.

Rossy jets through the air like a one-man plane.

FACT FILE

Yves Rossy's jet-wing

- Wingspan: 2.4 metres
- Engine: Four model aircraft jet engines
- Power: Unknown
- Top speed: 304 kilometres per hour
- Crew: 1

HOW FAST?

With his jet-wing, Yves Rossy can fly as fast as a racing car.

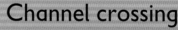

The jet-man returns to the ground by parachute.

Channel crossing

In 2008, Rossy used his jet-wing to fly across the English Channel. He made the crossing in only 9 minutes and reached 200 kilometres per hour. Later the same year, he flew over the Alps, a mountain range in Europe, at a top speed of 304 kilometres per hour.

Air racers

Air races were very popular in the 1920s and 1930s. They encouraged aircraft designers to produce new, faster and more advanced planes.

Seaplane races

The Schneider Trophy air races were for **seaplanes**. They attracted crowds of more than 200,000 people. The last Schneider Trophy race was held in 1931, when the United Kingdom won the trophy for the third time. The winning plane was a Supermarine S.6B with an average speed of 547 kilometres per hour.

A Supermarine seaplane is prepared for a race.

The Macchi M.C.72 was the fastest plane in 1933 and 1934.

Record breaker

The Italian Macchi M.C.72 racing seaplane was not able to take part in the last Schneider Trophy race because of engine trouble, but it went on to break the S.6B's air speed record twice. In 1934, it raised the record speed to 709 kilometres per hour.

A Supermarine S.6B starts its takeoff run.

FACT FILE

Macchi M.C.72

- Wingspan: 9.5 metres
- Engine: Fiat V24
- Power: 2850 horsepower
- Top speed: 709 kilometres per hour
- Crew: 1

HOW FAST?

The Macchi M.C.72 was twice as fast as a racing car at top speed.

War planes

No new air speed records were set between 1939 and 1945 because the world was at war. However, faster and faster aircraft were developed during World War II.

Fast fighters

The best fighters for air battles were lightweight and fast. By 1945, some fighters were flying faster than the record-breaking speeds set before the war. The Hawker Hurricane fighter had a top speed of 544 kilometres per hour. The famous Spitfire fighter and its rival, the Messerschmitt Bf-109, were even faster.

The Spitfire's top speed was more than 600 kilometres per hour.

Flying faster

During World War II, newer planes, such as the P-51D Mustang, were built. They were faster than the Spitfire. Later planes, such as the Corsair navy fighter, were even faster. The Corsair's top speed was about 718 kilometres per hour, but the age of fast planes with propellers was coming to an end.

Some Mustangs took part in air races after the war.

The Corsair's engine was the most powerful in the world in 1940.

FACT FILE

Vought F4U-4 Corsair

- Wingspan: 12.5 metres
- Engine: Pratt & Whitney R-2800 radial engine
- Power: 2450 horsepower
- Top speed: 718 kilometres per hour
- Crew: 1

HOW FAST?

At top speed, a Mustang or Corsair fighter could fly the length of two football fields in about one second!

First jet fighters

The first jet fighters were built in the 1940s, during World War II. They could fly far faster than planes with propellers.

Jet planes

The jet engine was invented in Britain by Frank Whittle in 1930, but Germany built the first jet plane. The German Heinkel He-178 made the first jet-powered flight on 27 August 1939. Germany also built the first jet fighter, the Messerschmitt Me-262. It had a top speed of 870 kilometres per hour. It was much faster than other fighters at that time.

The Heinkel He-178 was the first practical jet plane.

The Me-262 was the first fighter without a propeller.

A Gloster Meteor was the fastest plane in the world in 1945.

New records

The first British jet fighter was the Gloster Meteor. In 1945, a Meteor that had been **modified** to go faster than normal set the first air speed record after the war. It flew at 975 kilometres per hour. Air forces in different countries quickly changed from fighters with propellers to jet-powered fighters.

FACT FILE

Gloster Meteor
- Wingspan: 13.1 metres
- Engines: Two Rolls-Royce W.2B/23 Welland turbojets
- Power: 15,100 newtons
- Top speed: 975 kilometres per hour
- Crew: 1

HOW FAST?

The record-breaking Gloster Meteor was as fast as a jet airliner today.

Faster than sound

When pilots flew close to the speed of sound, their planes shook and became harder to steer. There was something strange about the speed of sound that plane-makers struggled to understand.

The sound barrier

Some people thought it might be impossible to fly faster than sound safely, so the **speed of sound** became known as the sound barrier. The first plane to break through the barrier was the *Bell X-1*. It was an experimental plane powered by a rocket.

The *Bell X-1* was shaped like a bullet.

The Super Sabre was the first U.S. supersonic fighter plane.

Sonic boom

On 14 October 1947, the *X-1* was carried into the air underneath a B-29 bomber. At a height of 6000 metres, the bomber dropped the *X-1*. Its pilot, Charles 'Chuck' Yeager, fired the rocket and the plane soared away. As the *X-1* went through the sound barrier, people on the ground heard a loud sonic boom. Supersonic (faster than sound) flight had arrived!

FACT FILE

Bell X-1

- Wingspan: 8.5 metres
- Engine: XLR11-RM3 rocket
- Power: 26,700 newtons of thrust
- Top speed: 1541 kilometres per hour
- Crew: 1

HOW FAST?

The *Bell X-1* was about five times faster than a racing car at top speed.

Concorde

In the 1950s, Britain and France started work on a new supersonic plane. It was to be a supersonic airliner, and it was called Concorde.

Concorde's nose was lowered to give a better view for landing.

Concorde could outfly most military jets because it could fly at supersonic speeds for several hours.

Working together

At first, Britain and France worked separately on different airliners. Later, they joined forces and worked together on the same project. They built a slender, white, dart-shaped plane. Concorde made its first test flight on 2 March 1969. It went supersonic seven months later and carried its first paying passengers on 21 January 1976.

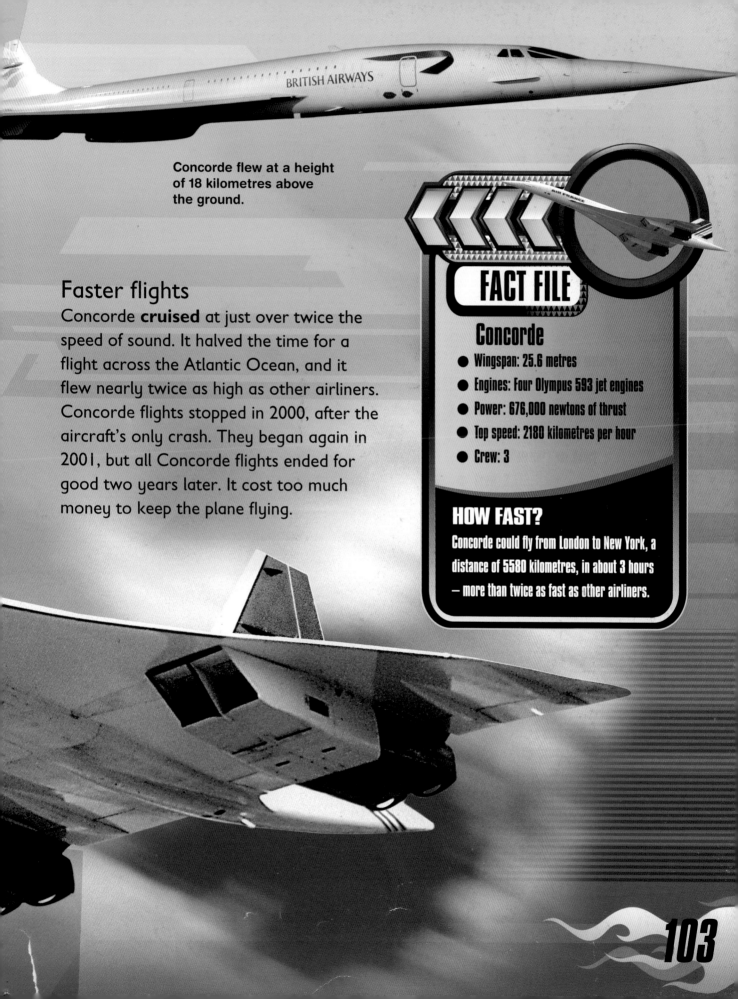

Concorde flew at a height
of 18 kilometres above
the ground.

Faster flights

Concorde **cruised** at just over twice the
speed of sound. It halved the time for a
flight across the Atlantic Ocean, and it
flew nearly twice as high as other airliners.
Concorde flights stopped in 2000, after the
aircraft's only crash. They began again in
2001, but all Concorde flights ended for
good two years later. It cost too much
money to keep the plane flying.

FACT FILE

Concorde

● Wingspan: 25.6 metres
● Engines: Four Olympus 593 jet engines
● Power: 676,000 newtons of thrust
● Top speed: 2180 kilometres per hour
● Crew: 3

HOW FAST?

Concorde could fly from London to New York, a
distance of 5580 kilometres, in about 3 hours
— more than twice as fast as other airliners.

Supersonic fighters

The first supersonic fighters were built in the 1950s. Today, fighters can easily fly at more than twice the speed of sound. They are about 150 times faster than the first aeroplane!

The Raptor is named after fierce birds of prey.

The fighting Raptor

The Lockheed Martin F-22 Raptor is the latest US fighter. It began its service with the US Air Force in 2005. Its top speed is just over twice the speed of sound. Planes like the F-22 are amazingly expensive. Each F-22 costs over US $100 million.

The F-22 Raptor has two jet engines.

Europe's fighter

The latest European fighter is the Eurofighter Typhoon. The first Typhoon was delivered to the German Air Force in 2003. Six air forces now have Typhoons. Plane-makers in Germany, the UK and Italy worked together to create the Typhoon. It has a top speed of nearly 2500 kilometres per hour. Tiny, **swivelling** wings on the plane's nose help it turn more tightly in air battles.

A Typhoon can weigh up to 23.5 tonnes.

FACT FILE

Eurofighter Typhoon

- Wingspan: 10.95 metres
- Engines: Two Eurojet EJ200 turbofans
- Power: 120,000 newtons of thrust
- Top speed: 2495 kilometres per hour
- Crew: 1

HOW FAST?

The Eurofighter Typhoon is more than twice as fast as an airliner.

Blackbird

In 1976, a plane called the Lockheed SR-71 Blackbird flew at 3529 kilometres per hour. This air speed record for manned jet planes has never been broken.

Spy in the sky

The Blackbird was a US Air Force spy plane. It flew so high and so fast that no enemy plane or missile could catch it. Its strange, flattened shape and special, black paint protected it, too. They were chosen to make the plane harder for an enemy to find by using **radar**. It flew thousands of secret missions from 1964 to 1998.

The Blackbird's nose contains spy cameras.

The Blackbird's tail fins lean inwards.

High flyer

The Blackbird flew at more than three times the speed of sound. It flew up to about 25,900 metres – more than twice as high as an ordinary airliner. In fact, it flew so high that the two crew members had to wear spacesuits. The Blackbird has now been replaced by spy **satellites** in space.

FACT FILE

Lockheed SR-71 Blackbird

- Wingspan: 16.9 metres
- Engines: Two Pratt & Whitney J58 jet engines
- Power: 290,000 newtons of thrust
- Top speed: 3529 kilometres per hour
- Crew: 2

HOW FAST?

The Blackbird flew four times faster than an airliner.

High-flying Blackbird pilots wore spacesuits.

Edge of space

Twenty years before the Space Shuttle started carrying astronauts into orbit in 1981, a rocket-plane was already flying into space. It was an experimental rocket-plane called the *X-15*.

Soaring away

The *X-15* could fly more than six times faster than sound, but it never held the world air speed record. To set a new record, an aircraft has to be able to take off by itself. The *X-15* was carried into the air underneath the wing of a B-52 bomber. The bomber dropped the *X-15* at a height of 13,700 metres. Then, the pilot fired the *X-15*'s rocket and soared away.

The *X-15* made a total of 199 flights.

The *X-15* was carried into the air by a bomber.

The *X-15* was powered by a rocket in its tail.

SpaceShipOne

In 2004, another rocket-plane dropped from a **mothership** flew to the edge of space. It was called *SpaceShipOne*. It was the first manned spacecraft developed by a private company, not a government agency. Its top speed was about 3500 kilometres per hour.

SpaceShipOne hangs below its mothership.

Space Shuttle

The Space Shuttle is nearly four times faster than the _X-15_. It has to reach a speed of about 28,000 kilometres per hour to go into orbit around Earth.

Boosting power

When the Space Shuttle takes off, the Orbiter vehicle with the astronauts inside is attached to two booster rockets and a huge tank of fuel. The fuel is burned by the three rocket engines in the Orbiter's tail. The engines and boosters provide the power needed to launch the Shuttle.

The Space Shuttle blasts off from its launch pad.

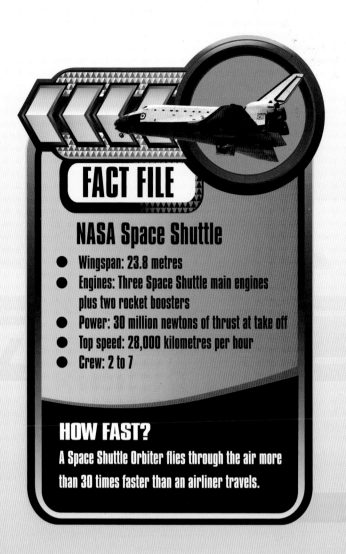

NASA Space Shuttle

- Wingspan: 23.8 metres
- Engines: Three Space Shuttle main engines plus two rocket boosters
- Power: 30 million newtons of thrust at take off
- Top speed: 28,000 kilometres per hour
- Crew: 2 to 7

HOW FAST?

A Space Shuttle Orbiter flies through the air more than 30 times faster than an airliner travels.

The Space Shuttle soars away from Earth.

Around Earth

When the fuel is used up, the fuel tank and booster rockets fall away. The Orbiter continues into orbit around Earth. At the end of its mission, the Orbiter slips out of orbit and returns to Earth. It re-enters the atmosphere at about 25 times the speed of sound.

The Orbiter lands like a plane on a runway.

United States

NASA

Apollo 10

The fastest craft ever to fly through the air with a crew was the command module of the *Apollo 10* space mission.

Moon mission

The *Apollo 10* spacecraft orbited the Moon for two months before *Apollo 11* landed the first astronauts on the Moon. *Apollo 10*'s job was to practice everything that *Apollo 11* would do, except land on the Moon. The spacecraft was made up of three parts: the command **module**, the service module, and the lunar excursion module. Only the command module landed back on Earth. The spacecraft was launched by a mighty *Saturn V* rocket, which was as powerful as 130 jet fighters.

The giant *Saturn V* rocket was as tall as a 36-storey skyscraper.

The Apollo spacecraft orbits the Moon.

The pull of gravity

As *Apollo 10* returned to Earth, the pull of Earth's **gravity** made it fly faster and faster. Astronauts Thomas Stafford, John Young and Eugene Cernan were inside the tiny spacecraft. As it plunged into the atmosphere, the command module was traveling at nearly 40,000 kilometres per hour!

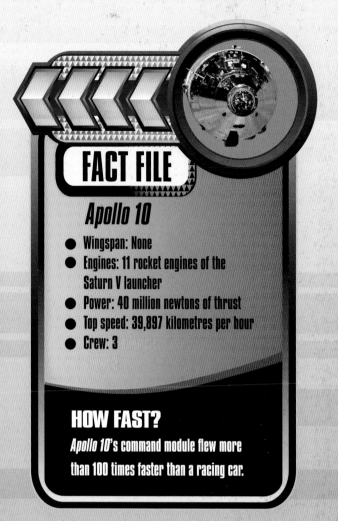

FACT FILE

Apollo 10

- Wingspan: None
- Engines: 11 rocket engines of the Saturn V launcher
- Power: 40 million newtons of thrust
- Top speed: 39,897 kilometres per hour
- Crew: 3

HOW FAST?

Apollo 10's command module flew more than 100 times faster than a racing car.

The *Apollo 10* Command Module landed in the ocean.

Future records

Aircraft that fly faster than five times the speed of sound are called hypersonic. Future hypersonic aircraft are being designed now.

Test flight

Some hypersonic aircraft will be able to fly 10 or even 20 times faster than the speed of sound. A small **unmanned** plane called the *X-51* will make test flights up to about seven times the speed of sound. Another unmanned aircraft called *X-43A* has already reached almost 10 times the speed of sound. It was fitted to a rocket hanging underneath a B-52 bomber. The bomber launched the rocket. Then the *X-43A*'s engine started and the plane soared away.

The *X-51* and its rocket are prepared for a flight.

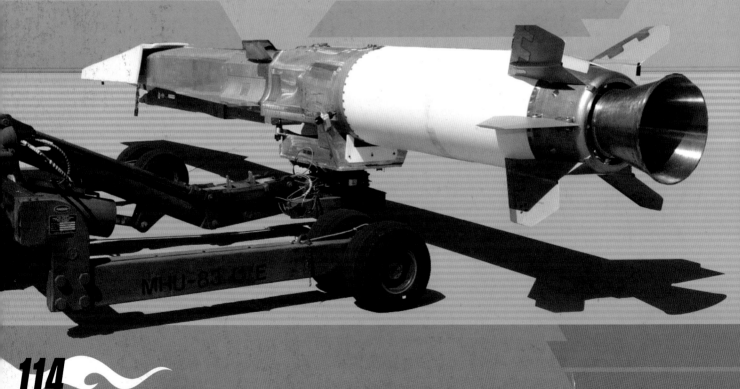

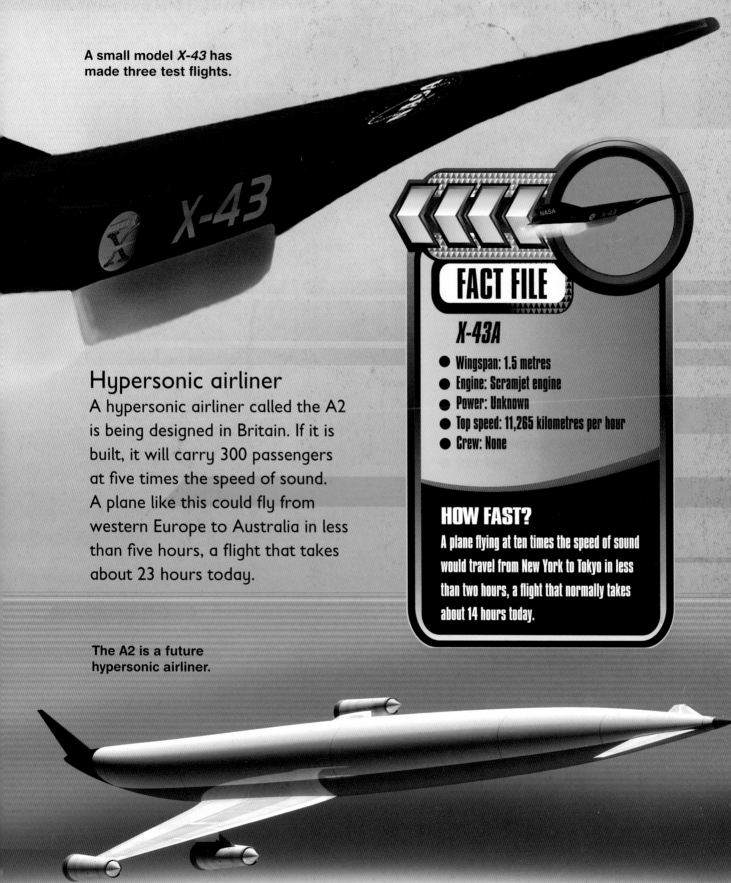

A small model *X-43* has made three test flights.

Hypersonic airliner

A hypersonic airliner called the A2 is being designed in Britain. If it is built, it will carry 300 passengers at five times the speed of sound. A plane like this could fly from western Europe to Australia in less than five hours, a flight that takes about 23 hours today.

The A2 is a future hypersonic airliner.

FACT FILE

X-43A

- Wingspan: 1.5 metres
- Engine: Scramjet engine
- Power: Unknown
- Top speed: 11,265 kilometres per hour
- Crew: None

HOW FAST?

A plane flying at ten times the speed of sound would travel from New York to Tokyo in less than two hours, a flight that normally takes about 14 hours today.

Glossary

anchored Held firmly in one place.

automatically Working on its own, without any need for someone to operate controls.

carbon fibre A very strong, lightweight material made from plastic, strengthened by strands of carbon.

cockpit The part of a boat, plane, or car where the driver, pilot or other crew members sit.

cruised Flew at the speed that burned the smallest amount of fuel.

designer A person who creates the shape and plans of how something, such as a car, operates.

diesel train A train pulled by a locomotive that is powered by a diesel engine.

ejection seat A rocket-powered seat that fires a pilot out of a military plane in an emergency.

electric car A car powered by one or more electric motors.

electric motor A machine that changes electricity into movement. Electric trains use electric motors to power their wheels.

engineer Someone who uses scientific and technical knowledge to design and repair machines.

experimental Built specially to test something new, such as a new shape of aircraft or a new type of engine, or to set a record.

fin A panel or surface that helps to keep a car going steadily in a straight line.

fireproof Able to resist fire. Fireproof clothing protects the person wearing it because it does not burn.

float A hollow, watertight part of a boat that floats on water.

gasoline engine An engine that burns gasoline inside it to produce power.

gravity A force that pulls everything down toward the ground. Aircraft have to overcome gravity to get off the ground and fly.

horsepower A measurement of the power of a machine, such as a car or boat.

hull The main part of a boat or ship that sits in the water.

hydroplane A very fast speedboat that sits on top of the water, instead of pushing through it like an ordinary boat.

jet engine An engine that produces a fast stream of hot air. The air is heated by burning fuel with oxygen from the air. The air expands and rushes out of the engine as a jet of hot air.

jet-car A car powered by a jet engine, instead of an ordinary car engine. The world's fastest cars are jet-cars.

jet-powered Pushed along by a jet engine.

land speed record The highest speed reached by a car on land.

launch system The mechanism that starts a roller coaster moving at the start of each run.

liquid natural gas (LNG) Gas that comes from under the ground and is then changed into a liquid. LNG can be burned in an engine to produce power.

locomotive An engine that moves under its own power and pulls trains.

missile A weapon powered by a rocket or jet engine that steers itself toward a target and then explodes.

model A copy of something, usually smaller than the real thing and sometimes built for tests.

modified Changed or adapted.

module A section, or part, of a spacecraft that is joined to other parts of the craft, but may be detached, if necessary.

mothership A plane, or spacecraft, from which a smaller craft is launched.

NASCAR The National Association for Stock Car Auto Racing.

official Believed to be true by an important organization.

propeller A device with long, twisted blades that spins fast to push a vehicle along or move a plane through the air.

prototype The first example of something to be built.

radar Stands for Radio Detection and Ranging. A system for detecting faraway aircraft by sending out radio waves and listening for any echoes that bounce back from the planes.

rocket A vehicle or engine that works by burning fuel with oxygen to produce a jet of gas that pushes the vehicle through the air. Unlike jet engines, rockets work in space.

rudders Flat sheets, or panels, that hang down behind boats and are turned to steer them.

satellites Spacecrafts that fly around Earth.

seaplane A plane with floats, instead of wheels, so that it can take off and land on water.

speed of sound The speed at which sound travels through something, usually 1236 kph. The speed of sound in air depends on how warm or cold the air is.

steam turbine engine A type of ship's engine that works by the power of steam produced by boiling water. A jet of steam makes a device called a turbine spin, which turns the ship's propeller.

streamlined With a shape that moves through the air as easily as possible, causing the least resistance to the air flowing around it.

supersonic Faster than the speed of sound. The speed of sound in air depends on how warm or cold the air is.

swivelling Turning or rotating.

titanium A strong, lightweight metal.

transatlantic Across the Atlantic Ocean.

turbine A drum with blades all around it. When a liquid or gas, such as a jet of steam, hits the blades, the drum spins. A turbine is part of a turbine engine.

turbocharged Boosted in power. A turbocharger is a machine that forces extra air into an engine, so it burns more fuel to give extra power.

unmanned Without any person or crew inside.

volt A unit of voltage or electric force.

Index